JUDY GRANT

The Power of Listening to Music

Why Music has a Language of its own

Copyright © 2024 by Judy Grant

All rights reserved. No part of this publication may be reproduced, stored or transmitted in any form or by any means, electronic, mechanical, photocopying, recording, scanning, or otherwise without written permission from the publisher. It is illegal to copy this book, post it to a website, or distribute it by any other means without permission.

Judy Grant asserts the moral right to be identified as the author of this work.

Judy Grant has no responsibility for the persistence or accuracy of URLs for external or third-party Internet Websites referred to in this publication and does not guarantee that any content on such Websites is, or will remain, accurate or appropriate.

Designations used by companies to distinguish their products are often claimed as trademarks. All brand names and product names used in this book and on its cover are trade names, service marks, trademarks and registered trademarks of their respective owners. The publishers and the book are not associated with any product or vendor mentioned in this book. None of the companies referenced within the book have endorsed the book.

First edition

This book was professionally typeset on Reedsy.
Find out more at reedsy.com

Contents

1. Introduction — 1
2. Why Do We Listen To Music — 3
3. What Are Some Of The Languages Songs Speak — 6
4. Music Says What You Are Not Able To Say — 9
5. Music Has The Ability To Soothe The Soul — 11
6. Will Every Song You Hear Lift You Up — 13
7. Why Music Has A Language Of Its Own — 16
8. What Makes Music So Powerful — 18
9. How Music Affects Trends, Cultures And The Way We Dress — 22
10. What Does Music Have The Ability To Do — 25
11. Conclusion — 27

1

Introduction

Hello and Welcome to The Power of Listening to Music: Why Music has a language of its own book. I am excited to write this book because looking over my life I'm reminded how much music has played a very big role in my life, and if you look back even now , you will see and hear music of all types and sounds all around you. Did you ever stop to think how music can really shape your life and your mood or attitude, or help you to push through a workout?

This book is what I have noticed through the lens of my life, while recognizing the significant role music will and can play in the life of everyday people.. Music has a life and language of its own and we will look at some of the things that music can add to a life as well as some of the things music can take away.

As we continue to explore the different types of music feel free to reminisce of the times music has taken your mind away and off of troubling situations or circumstances. Music is a great escape into rest and tranquil and calming sounds. Let's take a journey how music has shaped many situations and brought joy in others, for instance weddings. Let's think about workouts for a minute. The right song is so important, that it will determine whether you are able to complete or push yourself to the next level. Listening to a sad song white working out will totally drain all of your energy and you will feel like quitting, however, let's reverse that and put on a motivating song full of energy and Let's Go!! You got this!!

Now suddenly you find strength that you never had simply because you heard a good vibe that said you got this! Let's Go! You can do it!! Just a few more reps! It's really amazing when you look back over your life and you realize how songs began to control your mood, sometimes without your knowledge.

This is how music has a language of its own. Can you think of times where it was music that made the difference in a situation or circumstance? Follow me as we go through a few of them. As we began this book, think about how music and its language played a major or minor role in your life. May your music always lift you and take you to a tranquil place when you need to calm down and relax, and may music motivate you when you need that extra boost of energy.

2

Why Do We Listen To Music

Why do we listen to music? Music is able to completely cross all barriers of race, religion, countries and regions. There is no place you can go where music has not been. Music gives people temporary relief from life's troubling situations. The right song can have you dancing when you should be crying. So music provides a safe escape, even if you never left the room.

I listen to music because it is a great getaway, to a tranquil place full of rhythm and blues, songs that make you want to put on your dancing shoes. Music can soothe the soul and music can cause a sad day to be full of Joy.

Have you ever heard a song in your later years that you heard when you were a kid or a teen, young twenties and it took you back to summertime? You know those famous family and friend gatherings where music is playing in the park or back yard with the air being filled with the aroma of bar b que on the grill? The smell of barbecue in the air , as the sounds of music and laughter seem to be on the face of everyone enjoying the time spent together.

Picture this if you can, your song comes on, you were just about to grab you something to drink or eat , then the dj played that beat! You know that beat, that one that starts your body to moving before you are even ready to move? That beat that you just have to stop talking and put down your drink and food and say I have to dance, this is my song!!

So you get up and before you know it your family , friends and guests are all up like it's a dance floor, enjoying the beautiful breeze of summertime, feeling full of life as the beauty of fresh flowers sent the air, with trees that are so old but full of shade, just enough to keep the sun out your face. We listen to music because it is a great pick me up,and energy booster.

If you're like me sometimes you may feel so exhausted after working your full time job and taking care of and raising kids that you don't feel like all the other work that is waiting for you in the house. So what do you do? Well you have to get motivated because things will not take care of themselves. I go to my favorite radio station and turn it up! At first I start out just singing the lyrics to the songs, then I notice my energy level is starting to rise.

Now I'm cleaning my house with dance moves along the way. Have you ever been there? Every weight that I felt from work or being pulled in different directions just started to fade away and I"m now able to begin again, realizing that this too will pass and that each day is a blessing. After a few songs and meditation you realize that what made you upset doesn't even matter anymore, why?? Because listening to the right music has now put you in a positive space instead of a negative one.

We listen to music because the songs are saying something that is feeding us in some way. We listen to music because depending on the language it is speaking it can put us in the mood to do something different than we originally planned. Listening to music gives you that motivation to get together, share more, talk more, laugh more, while creating memories for life kinda vibe.

3

What Are Some Of The Languages Songs Speak

A few of the languages that music can speak, just to name a few are Love, Peace, Joy, Happiness, Anger, Sadness, Depression, Rage, and also Motivation. All of these languages can take on a life form of themselves left unchecked.

This is in no way all of the languages that music can speak, but just a few that I have noticed. So if you don't see your favorite language here, don't shoot the messenger lol. Love is a language often used in music. Love songs and worship songs are my favorite. I love songs that express love and unity that makes you feel like you're in the moment with the singer.There will be times when you just don't want to be bothered but when you hear that special song that reminds you of a special time automatically you begin to get a visual of a time before.

The right love song at the right time can be explosive and totally shift the whole atmosphere. Peace is a language that can be experienced by the tranquil waters flowing , or the sound of waves as you close your eyes to just take in the natural sounds of earth.

If you listen closely you will realize that everything around you is a song and has a melody. Listening to the flowing waters or the waves of the sea coming in, or easy listening music with soft sounds and smooth tones can not only calm your soul but help you to rest. Anger is another language that will play out into music, for example, have you ever been in an amazing mood and a song comes on the radio with dark sounds and the words are speaking and singing negative melodies about things that will only divide and place you in a negative mindset? Well after listening you find your mood shifting to anger and being irritated.

Yes, it is very important that we monitor how we hear and what we hear because these sounds are going into our gates called ears and will be feeding your soul and causing you to act out just because the sound isn't right. Sadness is another language of music. Have you ever listened to songs about somebody that was treated wrong or hurt in a relationship?

How did you feel after hearing it and repeating it over and over(the lyrics), can you remember how your mood changed to negative? Now you're wondering if it could happen to your situation. These are not healthy songs to meditate on because if you are able to relate to this, all of that vibrant energy you had will all drain out with that very song, make no mistake about it, some songs can steal from you. The language of confidence in a song can prepare you to do great things. While you are singing and doing the dishes and cleaning the house , now all of a sudden new business ideas began to drop, why?

You have now entered into a positive place where you are ready to receive and your soul is open to whatever the new task may be, and there is nothing at the time(negative) blocking your creativity that you have been blessed with. You have just entered a space where you just know that you can handle whatever comes.

The more you sing the songs confirming that nothing is impossible and nothing can stop your progress or break your stride, the more energy you put towards that goal knowing that you can do whatever you need to do to get to where you want to be. I'm gonna just give you one more, Happiness is a language that music speaks, if that beat is live and the words are positive it will pick you right up and turn your frown around to a smile.

Happiness and energy will cause you to flow and become creative in the things that you do, because there is no Debbie downer causing you to be depressed, you become encouraged and are sparked to succeed.

4

Music Says What You Are Not Able To Say

What is the benefit of old school music? Have you ever been in a situation where you wanted to tell your partner/spouse/girlfriend/boyfriend how you feel, but the words don't seem to come out of your mouth? Well you're in luck, old school music can say what you can't.

Every situation you have gone through, millions of people have gone through the same thing and some of them have put the words to a song that matches just what you want to say, which makes the whole mood flow in a loving way if done correctly. Music can set the whole atmosphere in church, home, dates, and workouts. Music and the words to the song can really make the difference between a loving evening and a boring evening. Music can totally shift the atmosphere no matter where you are.

Have you ever been dating someone for some time and things began to develop in a way you never knew it could, and now your emotions are involved and you want to express these words, but for some reason when you get in front of the person to say them, no matter how long you practiced the words in the mirror, the words never seem to come out.

You're listening to a song and suddenly you hear them expressing how you feel. You think to yourself, they had to have been where i am now or they wouldn't be able to describe what it's like to be in my situation and make it seem so clear, so what do we do? We are on a date or date night we set the mood, whether it's a nice dinner with candle light, with the lights dimmed and a very well prepared meal, then the icing on the cake you play that song that can say what you could not and the atmosphere is charged and now you feel relieved because the song just spoke for you.

5

Music Has The Ability To Soothe The Soul

The right song at the right time has the ability to create the right situation that can totally shift everything. Having a blue moment?, pop in a song that is full of energy and encouraging, suddenly you begin to come alive.

Where you felt so heavy, suddenly you are light and feel like getting outside and seeing something new. This is true for Gospel music as well, the right words at the right time can totally change your outcome and cause you to try again, or be patient knowing that God has already taken care of the situation, so you no longer have to dwell on the problem but you can look forward to what is coming, and have a thankful heart in the process while waiting and making melody in your heart.

There is nothing like the right song at the right time to give you that extra burst of energy that you need to enjoy the day. Meditate on what is good and lovely and positive. Breathing slowly in and out while listening to soft notes, easy listening, classical , jazz or just musical sounds on the instrument that cause you to relax.

Let's face it, we all need to rest and have many calm moments in our life. If you don't take the time to imagine where you want to go, or how it can change you and everyone around you, you probably won't get there without a plan. It's in those soothing times that your mind begins to get creative. Soothing sounds can cause you to rest when you used to be restless. Soothing sounds can totally take your mind off your circumstances and your situation and cause you to see your way clear.

If you like Worship music like I do, it can take you to another level, allowing joy to spring up like a well, not only soothing your mind but soothing your soul as well. Meditation on the right worship song is like elevation to your soul.

While letting you know who Jesus is, and what he has the ability to do . Nothing that you go through can ever stop you from getting to where you want to go. If you missed it , try it again tomorrow. Worship and begin to Love God for who he is. As you worship God , he will make his presence known and there will be a peace in your heart knowing God heard you.

6

Will Every Song You Hear Lift You Up

Absolutely not! You must be very selective of how you hear and what you hear because what you listen to is going to your soul (mind, will, emotions, thoughts). Listening to a song with low energy will drain your energy, while listening to a song with encouragement will make your heart glad and you can receive strength for the journey.

If listening to a song makes you angry or hate or want to fight? You may want to turn that off and assess what is happening to your emotions. Rule of thumb, what you pour in you will get out. If you are looking to be built up then you have to pay attention to what you are pouring in because you will begin to pick up attributes that you didn't have before.

One thing that is for sure music is everywhere you go, and not every song was created equal. Depending on the type of music and music style you like, will cause you to have a different view of things which everyone is entitled to their view. While music has been a very huge part of my entire life thus far I must conclude that all music isn't good to meditate on and listen to.

There are songs that we love, that we play over and over and over and what is that? It's a form of meditation and depending on the words that you are listening to will determine what you get out of the song, and it can also affect how you see things. Too much negativity breeds negativity.

If you want positive actions then you must put in positive things. Whatever a man sow that shall he reap. What fruit are you trying to produce? If good fruit, then listen to something that will not make you insecure or angry or sad or depressed. There are certain keys even on a piano that are definitely depressing! If you want to be encouraged and lifted and feel energized you may want to listen to something that can pull your energy level up and not down.

There are times even the beat of certain musical lyrics are counter productive to what you are trying to accomplish in your life and in your situation. When people go through certain hurts in life, and say for example they buried a family member and a certain song just brings them to depression because it keeps them stuck in the moment when the event occurred. It may not be wise to keep that particular song around you because of what it will trigger inside of you.

Every song will be different for different people, and what songs I like may not be your cup of tea, and that is ok because we were all made differently. We may come from different backgrounds, so we see through a different set of glasses.

Keeping an eye out on how something makes you feel may be a good feather to put in your hat. You are important and deserve to be loved and to be at peace. Remember and keep in mind what music that is playing in your ear is feeding your soul. Does this music inspire you, annoy you , make you angry, loving, peaceful or does it take away from you more than it's adding?

7

Why Music Has A Language Of Its Own

Music takes on many forms and shapes in our life. Old school, New School , classical, worship, praise, exercise, meditations and dance. Depending on the person listening to the song will determine the life that is given to it or that comes from the songs we listened to. The thing about the language of music, is it really doesn't need an interpreter because music is universal and there isn't a country or city ,state, nation, or part of the earth that has not been touched in one way or another from the sound of music.

Music still continues to speak from generation to generation day after day after day. Even babies relate to music. The Language of music transcends past cultural background and race and skin, it even goes past religion.

Music has been a part of this world from the very beginning and it continues to speak to many people in different ways, allowing them to express themselves through a language that fits their situation and circumstances. It doesn't matter if you're young, an infant or seasoned , music will speak to you in a way that others can't.

8

What Makes Music So Powerful

Music can help you meditate and focus, while bringing calmness to you're soul. Anything that can make you shift who you are and who you were is a very powerful tool. We as people don't realize sometimes the power of repetition. We as individuals must be aware that music can be positive or negative and very dangerous.

How can music become dangerous? If you notice you are becoming more and more angry, or slipping into depression or suddenly wanting to end it all or give up, then it will be wise to shift the song you are listening to and play something motivational or uplifting like a gospel or worship or some people like classical or just instrumental.(if you're not listening to a song but words that are negative in your thoughts, counter those thoughts by speaking the opposite positive thoughts your mind) Words of songs are very important, make sure they are giving you good positive vibes and not subtracting from your energy.

Music is so powerful because music has the ability to control your moods and attitudes. Music can pick you up or music will let you down. The right song will make you go one more hour in a workout when you are dog tired.

The right song at the hardest point of your lift has the ability to encourage you to keep pressing and keep pushing , while letting you know you got this , there is more in you than you realize. The right song can bring reconciliation to a people that have been distant. Anything that can change how you see, think , act is a powerful tool. Any time a song can motivate you, and cause you to rise up from where you are is a powerful song.

When a song can say what you can't and begin to patch things up, that is a power in itself. When a song can make you reminisce over what you had ,or have now that is a powerful song. When a song can cause you to forgive someone that you never thought that you could forgive, but you just happen to hear the right song at the right time, and when you heard that song you knew what you needed to do, that is a powerful song.

When you are in a good mood and just one wrong song can make you angry and cranky and not want to be bothered, that is a powerful song. If you are depressed and a song playing gospel or worship brings you back to yourself , then you have a powerful song. Growing up I heard songs about the blood of Jesus never losing its power, the blood that gives me strength , from day to day, it will never lose its power.

Songs about Salvation and the price that Jesus paid on the cross because he loved us so much, makes you want to surrender your life and recognize that you can't change you, and that you are nothing without him, and how much you really need him. That is a powerful song. If you can be in a marriage that is dying and you put on the perfect song that began to jog both of your memories, and you realize that what you were fighting over really doesn't matter and the fact that you are together now, and that you both have already overcome too many obstacles together that it would just not make sense to not work it out and enjoy the life that you both sacrificed to have, That is a powerful song.

If you can wake up in the morning and begin to worship and praise until the presence of the Lord begin to descend upon you, and now your whole atmosphere has changed? That is a powerful song.

If you can listen to a song and it causes you to love rather than to hate, make you rethink your ways and push through the many obstacles that can be in this life? That is a powerful song. If you can listen to the words of a song until tears began to fall down your face, not because you are depressed but because you are grateful that no matter what you went through, God's protection was all around you and he just wouldn't let you go, even when you no longer wanted to live?

And the right song came on and reminded you of all the reasons you need to keep going. That is a powerful song. If you can listen to a song and in the midst of the song see that what you said, what you did was wrong and not only acknowledge that it was wrong but make it right, because tomorrow is not promised to us, then that is a powerful song.

If you can wake up making melody in your heart, not because of what you did,or what anyone did but you are just grateful everyday because if it had not been for the Lord that was on your side you would be lost.

That song that you find yourself humming over and over that reminds you of just how far God has brought you? That is a powerful song. If you began to meditate and as you look back over your life you recognized that it was God that carried you all the time when you thought it was your own strength? That is the power of a song.

9

How Music Affects Trends, Cultures And The Way We Dress

Musical songs and videos have a huge influence on culture and trends even how some young adults dress and view themselves. Although it's not just the young adults, it's adults, kids and everyone in between.

People sometimes take their cues, and dress code after their favorite singer, song writer or video. Whatever hair style their favorite singer has and whatever the color is of their hair, you will find it becoming a trending thing because of the followers and following the artists have. Many people see themselves or imagine their life through their favorite artist and to some extent they copy as much of their life and lifestyle as possible (without the money they have of course).

You start seeing even the clothes and shoes that they were including jackets start to trend , in some cases even if they can't really afford to get it, sometimes it gives a sense of being a part of a trend, and when that shift to another trend people change with it just like changing a song from one song to another.

There are other groups (can be many groups of people) that love the music but they are secure and who they are and how they dress, so they are not swayed or moved by any peer pressure to have the latest shoes or jackets. Michael Jackson , the way he could dance and sing! People all over the Globe, the entire World began to imitate his dance moves , style of dress, shoes, jackets and the famous hat and gloves! Even doing the moonwalk! From the youngest to the oldest he was being duplicated.

When he came out, people were screaming and passing out, and simply overwhelmed with every emotion at the same time. His music went beyond anything political, racial and crossed so many barriers that people knew his name and face no matter where he went.

People didn't mind traveling and paying for high tickets, all because of the music and the artists creativity. People were brought together all over the world. Different Nations, cultures and all standing next to each other eagerly waiting to see what amazing sound or dance move or spectacular thing he would do. I must admit , I was tuned in as well and had my Michael Jackson Jacket and One white glove and every album he ever put out. When you really love a song or the artist that produces the song , you will go out of your way to support and even purchase what they have for the memory of the time you were there.

So music begins to cause memories in your mind, now every time you hear a song that was at the live concert you recall the whole atmosphere, the many people for that moment all on one accord wanting to get a glimpse of him or have him look in their direction, (even though thousands upon thousands were there)no matter which direction he looked, everyone felt like he saw them and they were the only one he looked at, or he pointed at them.

Many people passed out, others had to be carried out. People can often take bits and pieces of others lives that they look up to and live their life through them. Whatever the artist endorse, they flock right to the store to get it because their favorite artist wore the same type of glasses, shoes and jackets. What the artist like and the restaurant they like to visit, you will see the music lovers also frequent the same place hoping that one day he will stop in while they are there.

Famous musical artists have a huge responsibility because so many are looking up to them and even dreaming of doing what they do because of the influence they have on the culture, fashion world and they are trend setters. If he wore his clothes backwards do you realize how many people all over the world would wear their clothes backward? Just food for thought.

10

What Does Music Have The Ability To Do

Music has the ability to feed the soul. The right song has the ability to bring laughter and joy in a crying situation. Music has the ability to let you express yourself in a safe space, that though you can't say what you are really thinking because for some they may get offended you can just let the music speak and the song go into all the places where you were denied access.

Having a song that you feel connects with your emotions can be soothing but also it can help to release the stress that has your shoulders all in a knot. If you allow the songs to enter the place that you may have felt there was no hope then the right song can point you in the direction of where your hope should be and how that hope will be an anchor for your soul.

Music has the ability to make you go the last mile when you couldn't even go a block. Music has the ability to refresh your mind and your thoughts while helping you locate where you are emotionally? Are there still hurts in the place that should have been healed? Why does this particular song make you sad or make you cry? Why does listening to songs of good relationships bring tears or joy? Music has the ability to locate you and find exactly where you are in your soul.

Even in the church the worship has a way of peeling back the hard layers so that your heart will be open even in the midst of the rough surface and exterior and mental toughness that we continue to show on our way to healing.

Worship has the ability to lay your heart bare before the Lord so that he will restore what you humbly bring before him. Music has a way of making conversations easy that would be difficult to have, by changing the atmosphere in the room. As the saying goes about the Elephant in the room ?

So is tension that is so thick that you can cut it with a knife. You can feel that the space you are in is peaceful or if it is off. Music can turn an awkward situation into a fruitful and loving situation. Music can have love flow or it can cause hate to flow depending on what it is that you choose to listen to .

11

Conclusion

In conclusion it is very important to the soul that we feed ourselves with things that will build us rather than tear us down. Music that will help us to love rather than to help us hate.

Songs that will aid in our growth rather than to take us backwards on the wrong path. While listening and focusing on the songs, pay close attention to what the words are saying, how does it alter my mind, will and emotions? Does this make me better or worse? Is it really worth arguing over or should we go our separate ways? Can this known language help me to express myself in a positive way while helping me to get into shape so that I can live a productive life.

When I am listening to my easy listening music, classical, jazz , Love, summertime ballads am I at ease or does it make me anxious? Is what I am pouring into my soul helpful or hurtful? Will this music give me positive vibes or cause me to see all men in a certain light that I will never end up in a relationship because I have allowed music to build the wrong mind set in my heart?

Do I really believe I am able to do what I put my mind to do! If I put this energized song on can I stay focused enough to complete those tasks that will pile up if I don't? Does what I am singing line up with where I want to go? Am I taking the time for myself to unwind and refresh? If I'm not and I become depleted, who can I help? Am I being intentional when I began to worship and praise and meditate? What can I incorporate in my daily lifestyle that will help me get the desired results that will take me to the next level or the next dimension?

We often think that it doesn't matter what music we listen to or how we hear but everything that we put into our ears is a result of the life we now live. If you travel back down memory lane you can see that what you meditated on, you now live that life and lifestyle.

No need to wonder, how did I get here, you got here by what you heard, either by growing up as a child, hanging with friends in young adulthood, or through the place or places you have worked and lets not forget the relationship aspect of it. Just like music our life is playing its own melody and it is singing songs of things to come. It would be very beneficial if everyone, pay attention to mood swings themselves. Am I where I want to be?

How can I get to where I want to be if I am here? Am I consistent with my daily plans? What should I meditate on that will help me stay positive in the times we are living in? The Power that music has is endless and if you have listened to it at any length of time then you already know that it has shaped you too.

I hope that this book allows us to always be conscious of our moods and when they swing and shift and what was I doing when this began to take place, and then take action, began to meditate on what is good , lovely

CONCLUSION

and of a good report and go and get your joy back if you lost it and let it overflow if you still have it. Music Is powerful because it is a tool that will get results.

May the music fill your life like a sweet melody and may the sweet rhythm begin to soothe your soul like a sweet melody. Always make time to unwind, refresh and revive the time and life you have left , love those around you and be kind and wise. I hope there was something in these pages that gave you encouragement and an insight on ways music can work hand in hand to help you achieve your goals. Have a wonderful life full of love and joy, until we meet again God Bless.

I really hope you have enjoyed this book as much as I enjoyed writing it! And that it has helped you to see music in a different light or maybe even appreciate music a little bit more than before. If you found this book helpful, I'd be very appreciative if you left a favorable review for the book on Amazon. Thank you for reading it.